TRIUMPH HOUSE
Poetry with a Purpose

IN SILENT PRAYER

Edited by

Kelly Deacon

First published in Great Britain in 2000 by
TRIUMPH HOUSE
Remus House,
Coltsfoot Drive,
Woodston,
Peterborough, PE2 9JX
Telephone (01733) 898102

HB ISBN 1 86161 713 5
SB ISBN 1 86161 718 6

FOREWORD

Poetry is a creative art now becoming more widely received and recognised. Many people are now taking an interest in this special gift and using it to express their deepest feelings and emotions.

In Silent Prayer is a collection of over 130 writers who have joined hands to bring their feelings and emotions together, offering a great wealth of inspiration and insight into the Christian Faith.

This anthology is a true friend for life and will be a treasured reading companion for many years to come.

Kelly Deacon
Editor

CONTENTS

GIFTS

Give me Knowledge
And I have the stones to pave
  The way to Fame,

Then give me Wealth
And I have what all do crave
  Plus an honoured name.

But without Love
Each is like a tiny cloud
  In a boundless sky;

Withhold me Love -
Then give me a coffin and a shroud
  And let me die!

Theresa Manville

In The Stillness

In the stillness
Is where I find you God.
In amongst the troubles
And traumas
Of everyday life.
There, beyond the noise and
Distractions
Through the superficiality of life
I struggle
To keep my head above water,
To search and find
My moment of paradise
Where You wait for me.

How do I dare defy
You, Lord?
Creator, Holy One, Prince of Peace.
Father.
How dare I let days,
Hours, minutes, seconds
Steal past me,
And with them, precious time
With You.
Why does it seem almost too much
To part with?
To give you my all?
To sacrifice.

Above the resilient
Noise of busyness and
Heartache and jealousy
And selfishness and pain
And helplessness
And despair and
Sadness

Is a small voice
Calling out my name. In love.
Reaching out for
Me.
Yet I keep on ignoring.
Living my life. My way.

How sad that I have
Felt his gentle touch
Heard His soft voice
And once myself surrendered
In His awesome presence.
But I will strive
To reach that place
Again to be with You
To know that peace
Beyond understanding.
To radiate that happiness
Stemming from Your divine stillness.

To be the person I know
You desire me to be.
To be a child of God.

Nathalie Kusicka

Keep Pretending

Deep down I suffer within,
No form of release,
My emotions are trapped in sin,
Too hard to pretend,
It's clear that nobody can win,
When they hurt.

Looking into the faces that hurt,
Is like a mirror,
Into the anguish within my heart,
Not only actions and words,
But all the time being kept apart,
How can time heal.

All the pain time could try to heal,
If you let it go,
But all the heartache could kill,
As it is everything,
That I taste and touch and feel,
Life is ending.

Life seems to be coming to an ending,
As my heart shatters,
It's so hard to keep pretending,
That it doesn't hurt,
The world and reality are bending,
To allow more pain.

Stacey Davis

My Prayer

Dear father, please listen to my prayer
Give me a sign to show how you care
Keep watch over my husband and family
They are the ones that mean so much to me

Bless all those in trouble and suffering from stress
They need you so much Lord, their lives are a mess
Please take care of them in your own special way
And guide them through to another day

In times of illness please God be there
And take from our shoulders the burden we bear
Thank you dear Lord for all that you do
Our lives would not be the same without you.

Marjorie Ridley

JOIN HANDS

Join hands and share the beauty
Of these wondrous gifts from heaven.
To keep peace all around us
Then wrong doings be forgiven.

Look out now for your neighbour
Always show a helping hand.
Be there for one another
Let them know you understand.

Spreading the word he taught us
Granting patience each new day.
That we may travel safely
Brightly shine the light alway.

Hold onto faith forever
With such love deep in your heart.
Hope also walk beside you
Then much goodness to impart.

Together in one family
Then never alone to be.
Enrichment in your glory
Great blessings eternally.

Margaret Jackson

UNTITLED

(Phil.4:6)

Be anxious for nothing but in everything by prayer
And supplication with thanksgiving let your requests
be made known to God

As we face today Lord
please keep us in your care
Lord in our darkest hour
we ask you hear our prayer
let your spirit guide us
through every waking hour
bringing love and healing
through Your almighty power

Ann Langley

Always Near

I turn to you O Lord in prayer
Because I know you're always there
Always there both night and day
Ready to listen whenever I pray

I turn to you when I'm in doubt
You always help me sort it out
Help to ease my troubled mind
Through my prayers - this I find

Little things from day to day
Show me you're not far away
I know you always will be there
For this I thank you Lord - in prayer.

Vivien Holden

Daily Prayer

Aim each day, to be with God
Make each day to be for God
Exalt the truth, by faith in God
Nought come between yourself and God.

Geof Farrar

WHEN THE DAY HAS ENDED

When the day has ended and darkness starts to fall,
Let the silence stimulate a deeper thought of what has been
And what's to come,
Begin each day anew, renew what we could and should have done,
Remembering those irritations, the look of scorn, the time that
Could be better spent.
Open up the inner you, ready to approach the new day when it comes,
More understanding empathy, thought for others and their
Points of view.
With guidance from above help these missions, all come true,
Learning every day, why we are here and what we have to do,
Correct mistakes, banish mistrusts bringing in forgiveness
With help from above for each day and every day.
I thank you for those ups and downs from which we learn and grow,
Becoming more worthy for the day we'll one day live with you.
Amen

Liz Dicken

My Prayer

Thank you God for all your love,
Thank you God for heaven above,
Thanks for all we see and hear,
Thanks for all that we hold dear,
We thank you for the trees and flowers,
For grass so green and April showers,
Keep us Lord within your care
Ever loving our lives to share,
Help us to love him above and others
And all people on Earth as sisters and brothers.

Sinnelly

A Prayer For A Friend At Night

We'll say a prayer for you tonight
And know that God has heard.
We know the answer in our hearts,
We trust His sacred word.

We ask that He'll be near you
As each new day comes by -
To give you health and happiness
And strength from Him on high.

We ask for peace to light the way
In all things, great and small.
We ask Him for His loving care
And presence best of all.

Gwilym Beechey

LORD, SHINE YOUR LIGHT

Lord, shine your light on me,
Uncover all that is not true.
Sweep clean my heart
And make me more like you.

Thank you for all the blessings
You shower upon me every day.
Thank you for my family and friends
Make me a blessing to them, I pray.

As I go to sleep tonight
May I rest in your love.
Although I cannot see you I know you are there,
I feel your care and your peace from above.

Cathy Mearman

MEDITATION

I gaze into the candle flame
And pray your love will brighter burn.
That men from war their thoughts will turn
And peace will reign under your name.

I gaze into the firelight glow
And pray for countries far away,
Where floods and famine hold their sway:
That peoples there your help will know.

I gaze into the sea so blue
And pray the homeless beds will find:
That injured souls your hand will bind
And faithless ones will learn from you.

I gaze into the sky above
And pray for strength to face this day:
That unkind thoughts will flee away
When met with your undying love.

I gaze into the night so still
And pray my love for you will grow:
That others see and come to know
Their emptiness your grace can fill.

Jennifer Stella Smeed

A Prayer Fur Aw Things

Gie me a hailthy stamach, Lord,
An' sumwhit tae digest.
Gie me a hailthy bodie Lord,
An' keep it as its best.
An' gie me a hailthy mind Lord,
Tae be claen in Yer sicht.
Gie me a scunner at sin Lord,
An' stren'th tae dae whit's richt.

Gie me a mind that isna boun,
That disna whumper, souch or sigh.
Dinna lat me wirry muckle,
Aboot the funny wan cawed 'I',
Gie me a guid sense of fun Lord,
An' gie me wut tae see a baur.
An' git sum blythness oota life,
Tae pass it on like a new staur.

George Pritchard

Keep My Eyes On Jesus

I must keep my eyes upon Jesus
For if I turn away
Things of the world will come crowding in
Dimming my view of His face.
If I turn from Jesus, Satan will be there
Ready to do his utmost, sowing doubt and fear.

I must keep my eyes upon Jesus, nothing must come between
My love for Him my worship, more on Him I must lean
For Satan's always ready, each time I look away
He uses situations I meet with every day.

His weapons do not matter, He has one end in view
To turn my eyes from Jesus, His methods are not new
But nothing really matters, discord may be there
I must keep my eyes upon Jesus and trust more in His care.

Jesus is stronger than Satan and sin
With Him on my side each battle I'll win
Each storm which assails me, each doubt and each fear
Will go as a cloud when Jesus is near
I trust in His promise, I know He will keep
Me safe from temptation, His face I must seek.

I cannot fight with Satan, unless I really know
That Jesus is beside me my Saviour and my Lord
The lessons that God teaches are costly and I know
I must turn my back on Satan and only Jesus know.

There must be no chinks in my armour
Where Satan can get in
I must arm to fight the battle, if I shall victory win
With truth and love and patience, be faithful
For I must keep my eyes upon Jesus
And fully on Him trust.

I know 'twas for me he suffered and died
Yet so perfect was He
He'll help me and guide me in all that I do
I now it really is true.
I know Jesus loves me my wonderful Lord
His promise I truly believe
I know I can trust Him, I know He loves me
I know it really is true.

Dorothy Swann

DIANA LAMENT

O Thou above in heavens high
To whom we oft sing aloud in praise
We cry louder now - alas - in lament
With out fair Diana laid at rest.

An English rose truly above the best
Little wonder then she became our dear Princess
That filled our cruel world with but kindness
Yet our beloved lies cold in death.

From her heart the love poured out free
Among world's poor of all nationality
Such faith and hope against misery
And with hands on even if leprous be.

Yet in seeking self happiness
How cruel the hand of fate to she
The hounds of Hell bay'd her death knell
And thus we cry aloud to Thee.

And as loud and louder still we sing
The tears flow in constant stream
The angel of love you sent to earth
Within thy boson again doth rest.

Gilbert

POETIC PRAYERS

Though I am weak and lowly,
You are, ever near,
And even when, I have sinned,
You still, want to hear,
For You are with me ever,
You, are with me now,
Lord, please don't deny me,
As my head, I bow.

Evelyne A McMaster

A Prayer For Our Families

Lord, we thank You for our families,
All the people we hold dear;
Father, mother, sister, brother,
Relatives both far and near.

Lord, direct our life together,
May Your love rule all we do;
Trusting, caring, giving, sharing,
Young and older, pleasing You.

Lord, forgive our selfish actions,
Hurtful words; and may there be
Patience showing, kindness growing;
Help us live in harmony.

Lord, we bring to You our families;
In our joys and sorrows share.
Be our mother, father, brother;
Bless us now, and hear our prayer.

Rosemary Platt

Inner Strength

To feel the wind in my hair
Soft rain upon my face
Are all the things I ever need
To keep me in my place

The warm winds caress my back
Sweet scents my senses fill
Give me the strength to face each day
And command me to do thy will

Meash

HEAVEN

I want to go to Heaven
And see the angels fly,
And wave to me with kindness
As they gracefully pass by.

I want to feel the clouds surround
My body safe and warm,
And see the earth beneath me
In a very different form.

I want to breathe the air so clean
Unspoiled from carelessness,
And protect myself from honesty
Love and righteousness.

I want to speak of greater things
Recognise what's right from wrong.
And what can be accepted
So I know that I'll belong.

I want to go to Heaven
Where no longer will I fall,
I want to go to Heaven
The safest place of all.

Vivienne Bern

To Thy Unwavering

On knees proud,
We steep, before Pre-eminence.

Where lies discomfort,
When soul, bathing;
In Thirstlessness.

We of humbler mould,
Reap of completion;
In sip,
Of Maturity.

Dare not!
Avaricious spirit;
Lead.

Passions propel, fleshy fashion,
Towards desperation;
Lamentable, retrogression.

Having deemed wisdoms,
Eternal:
Succumb;
Where lies role,
In hesitancy?

On knees proud,
Spiritual emancipation,
Should arrive;
In faith.

We give of ourselves,
To thy unwavering,
Righteousness.

Rowland Warambwa

He Died

Our Lord died for you and me,
He bore the cross to Calvary,
He died of love for you and me,
He died a death of agony.
He died that we might be forgiven,
He died to make us good,
He died that we might go at last,
To be with Him in heaven above.

His blood was shed,
His tears were few,
He died to bring good news,
He died to set us free from sin,
To bring us life anew.

So Lord, I come to You this day,
There is no other way,
To praise, and thank, and bless You Lord,
But most to give You glory.
This is the truth, the light, the way,
It's not a made up story -
That Christ did die on Calvary,
But now He reigns in glory.

Jean Thornton

LOOK UP!

Think not to tread life's weary path
With dismal thoughts
And down-turned eyes.
Instead look up! Look up!
To marvel at the magnificence
Of God's skies.

Stand and absorb his heavenly love.
Sit and enjoy his comforting light.
Then rejoice!
That Jesus Christ his son was born,
To put our world right.

Diane Moules

STRETCH OUT A HAND

As I walk along life's road,
You are walking there beside me,
When I am looking for support,
Your hand reaches out to find me,
Your love comforts me,
Your faith guides me,
Through all the tears of sorrow and pain,
Your light comes down to brighten and warm me,
So God, when people ask me why I believe,
Of which they quite often do,
I can say with my hand on my heart,
Why shouldn't I, wouldn't you,
If you felt that glow of comfort and support,
When you were feeling as low as I do,
Then you would know his love is all around,
It's up to you to stretch out a hand and ask for help,
As I do.

Valerie Ann Kitchener

God's Almighty Care

Holding hands together
Let's kneel to say a prayer
Wishing love and happiness
To all when life's unfair,
Helping them believe
Whatever lays out there
God's spirit's always watching
He surrounds us, everywhere.
Let's pray for all their doubt
When the tunnel, has no end
It seems to run forever
There's light you can depend,
To pull you from a darkness
God's help, his strength, we send
To guide you through your blindness
Heaven once again.
Pray for all the children
Starting little lives,
Growing to the future
Their battle to survive,
Enjoying all the fruits
Eventually they reach
Take from Eden's garden
God's love, to hold and teach.
The beauty of our world
It's here for all to share
Look within the boundaries,
With compassion, and with care
Holding hands together
Our father, let us pray.

Martin Toyne

Requiem

Do not buy a corner of the earth for me
for I shall move, free spirit, across the seas
and mountains, drinking in the glories of the earth,
at last adrift from this life's history.

I'll watch the sunrise from a hundred places,
hobnob with a star or two, and when
I've had enough of cosmic wandering
I'll settle near a wise kind spirit elder
to learn what this past life,
despite its hard enduring lessons,
has still not tutored me.

And while you're scattering my ashes
in some quiet lovely place,
I'll waft across the scene and hope
my disembodied spirit
will take the sadness from your faces
and let you know that I am free,
happy to move on, and thankful too,
at having had the joy of knowing you.

Rachel Silbert

A Nightly Prayer

Tonight as I place my hands together
I pray thee Lord love me forever
I ask of you to forgive my sins
And keep me safe as the day begins
I ask of you, watch over those I love so dearly
I pray to you love them eternally
My faith for you exists in my heart
Without your love I'd fall apart
Please guide me on what path to take
And mend my heart when it does break
Give me faith and the strength to see
The good that exists inside of me
I ask of no riches, fame or wealth
Only for your love and my family's health
I pray you'll keep a place in heaven for me
To live life after death for eternity
Please take care of those in heaven above
The ones I've known and still cherish with love
I pray to you each and every night
To stay by my side and guide me right
Throughout my life however long that may be
And take my soul to paradise, forever, eternity
Amen

Kim Darwell

God As Near As Our Prayer

Quest of all ages your love never ends,
Light of the world, our continual care;
Your life is victorious, blessing friends.
Though distant, all are one through prayer.
Immortal God we see you in the Cross,
Where our self-worship and false pride is dross.

Seeking Shepherd of the wandering sheep,
You find in us both unbelief and doubt.
Our earthbound indulgence we strive to keep,
We struggle with conflicts within without.
Darkness comes, turning our backs to your light;
Sun of righteousness you make all things bright.

Earth's Galilean Lord of timeless truth,
Triumphed o'er death that no state might could gain.
Christ made the weak strong, gave ardour to youth.
In resurrection power Jesus shall reign.
Providential Guide setting people free,
We serve your goal of one fraternity.

Author of faith, eternal joy fulfil;
In despair's dark night your silent stars shine.
Free pardoning grace, strength unspeakable,
Your loving kindness, thoughts and deeds refine.
Your risen healing life is victory,
Quelling terrorised crimes with chivalry.

Blest Creator with heaven's host we sing,
Binding broken hearts in deep harmony.
For loved ones far away our prayers we bring,
Grant them your guidance, faith and company.
So shall earth's people with ten thousand tongues,
Praise you God of glory with thankful songs.

James Leonard Clough

SUNDAY SCHOOL PRAYER

There is someone who we call God who lives up high in heaven
In just six days he made the world and rested on day seven
He made the seas, the skies, the stars and he made you and me
And that's why we give praise to God in Christianity
So every day make someone laugh and make them want to smile
And when you see their happiness you'll find it's worth your while
Remember to be nice to all and spread a little fun
And then you'll earn your place with God and Jesus Christ, his son

Adam Sean Tormey

FROM A TREE IN MOZAMBIQUE

The water rises high dear Lord
I climb the swaying tree
Higher by the minute it comes
What's to become of me

My stomach hurts dear Jesus
I creep higher and cling tight
The hours go by and darkness falls
Oh! Help me in my plight

You sent us blight and hunger Lord
And still I trust in thee
Now it's floods to flush us out
But thank you for the tree

The pain is bad my Trinity
I push and hear a cry
I see a large bird droning loud
Circling round the sky

Then from the stomach of the bird
You're descending slow dear Lord
Within your arms at last I'm safe
You cut my baby's cord

The big bird comes from Britain you say
To pluck me from the tree
I bless their kind, compassionate hearts
They sent their love through thee

Monica Jackson

He's Not All Bad

I pray, my Lord, you're listening
He really deserves a break
No one's prepared to fight for him
But he's got just what it takes.
He knows he's done wrong in the past
And he's really paid the price
But please, Lord, give him a chance
It really won't happen twice.
I know that I'm no angel
I, too, have done things wrong
But he gave me the strength to realise
That I really do belong.
Lord, all I'm asking of you
Is to find it in your heart
To forgive him, to let him live again
And to let him play his part.
So please Lord, I ask this favour
You may not even give him a glance
But he really deserves a future
And we all deserve a chance.

Margaret Ann Scott

May All Have Peace In Heaven

You have my deepest sympathy,
And my condolences I send.
It's hard to lose someone you love,
So I think
Of you
My friend.

I know how much you love him,
In mind I will be there when you cry.
I, also, think of him,
Sleeping
On the clouds
In the sky.

May all have peace in heaven.

Janice Tucker

My Personal Prayer

Blessed Father hear my prayer I plead to bind this broken heart,
May thy spirit warm and tender touch my ever aching heart.
Would thou turn away this soul who entered into sin?
Oh no, sweet Father let that not be and let thy spirit in.

To heal, to mend this broken heart all troubles to thee I bring,
Dear Father now let my heart be light and ever let it sing,
Praises unto thee dear Lord, my ever-loving king,
Who hears and loves me to the end lift me with healing wings,
Up to the heavens, I hope to be, evermore to live with thee,
My Saviour hear my daily prayers and thy spirit be with me.

Amen.

Topsy Pass

GIVE ME YOUR LOVE

Here, in this world, we are but weary guests.
Wandering, lonely, without rest.
(With various pains and quite alone)
Far from our dear . . . and heavenly, home.

The stony paths show . . . no way to go.
I pray to You . . . the words won't flow.
I stumble, sometimes lose my way
So need a friend, a halt and stay.

Dear Lord . . . be Thou my centre-point.
I turn to You . . . on You I count!
When every joy in life is gone . . .
Give me Your love . . . to rest upon.

Brenda Robson-Eifler

In My Prayers

These are my prayers just for you
Because I think I know what is wrong with you
So I will pray to God to keep you safe
Until I see you again tomorrow.

These are my prayers just for you
Yet it does not matter if I get caught
Because in God my parents do not believe
For he is something they cannot see
To answer all their questions.

These are my prayers just for you
Until it is time for us to meet again
In our safe quiet place
When I will find if God has kept you safe
Enough to tell me that you love me
And that one day all my dreams will come true.

Keith L Powell

CHILDREN'S PRAYER FOR CREATURES RARE

If I were an untamed, roaring lion
Out there in the wild,
I'd growl ferociously at you
But I'd never harm a child.
If I were such a powerful beast
I'd thank the Lord each day
For all my strength and fearless courage
To keep enemies at bay.

If I were a tiny, squeaking mouse
Running round your loft,
I'd eat the titbits that you dropped -
I'd soon grow tame and soft.
If I were such a harmless mouse
I'd thank the Lord each day
For providing such a store of food
I'd always want to stay.

If I were a swaying elephant
Out in jungles green,
Munching leaves so peacefully -
I hide from hunters mean.
If I were such a hefty brute
I'd thank the Lord each day
That He has kept the hunters of
The ivory trade away.

If I were a purring Persian cat
Curled up by the fire,
I'd groom my fur and look so fine -
Of life I'd never tire.
If I were such a pampered cat
I'd thank the Lord each day
That He has found me comfort now
When once I was a stray.

Sylvia Price

Last Request

If I die in the summer; let it be here,
As the sun softly sinks 'neath the sky blue and clear.
If I die in the summer; let me be free,
For a last little dip of my toes in the sea.
If I die in the summer; let it be warm,
Let the sea breeze envelop my bodily form.
If I die in the summer; let it be clear,
To share the far view with my love, true and dear.
If I die in the summer; let it be dusk,
Like a curtain that falls on the things of the past.
If I die in the summer; let it be calm,
To hear the waves break to the 23rd psalm.
If I die in the summer; here on the sand,
May I walk to my heavenly end, hand in hand.

Beverley Seaby

The 'Teach Me' Prayer

Teach me the wisdom to express
My sorrows if in dread distress
And not to shy away in fear
When life itself becomes unclear!
I need to bend, to yield, submit . . .
If I'm to find some sense in it,
For life's not always 'right as rain' -
Despite God's sunshine, I've known pain . . .
I've seen my share of heartaches, too,
When only Jesus pulled me through!
Teach me to keep things simple, please . . .
Before life brings me to my knees!
The world is busy, super slick . . .
I'm not that fast; I'm not that quick . . .
Perhaps I should be . . . I don't know -
I'm not like others: on the go!
I need my space, some time to rest . . .
The search for cash is not my quest . . .
I'd rather find some self-control
Than sell my one eternal soul!
Teach me to treasure wholesome thoughts,
Avoiding heartless cold retorts
And spurning gossip overheard -
That goes against God's Holy Word . . .
It doesn't matter, false or true . . .
Why should I judge what others do?
I'm not much better than the rest!
If not for grace, I'd not be blessed!
God grant me faith, to pause and pray
With cause to 'Praise the Lord!' each day!

Denis Martindale

Imogen Fern

Thank you for this child of mine
Meek and gentle, so divine.
Sent from God to me on Earth,
Now I can celebrate her birth.

Tiny fingers, tiny toes,
Rosebud lips, button nose.
Thank you for this child of mine
Meek and gentle, so divine.

Fiona Nicholls

BEFORE I SLEEP

Thank you for my bed Lord
My warm and cosy home
For the gift of family and friends
So I don't walk alone
Forgive me the ungrateful days
When nothing at all seems right
Bless the homeless in a cardboard box
Under hedges and bridges in dead of night
Comfort the lonely, restore the lame
The sinner and the preacher
You love them all the same

Vicki Turner

My World

If we only had the answers
To 'peace' throughout our world.
If, we lit a 'tiny' candle,
Would our sick then all be healed.
If we showed some human kindness
To those who'd gone astray,
Then our lives would be much richer
There'd be 'hope' for us today.

There's a beautiful bright sunrise,
In a tropic land so far.
We can 'go there' if we want to,
By sea or air or car.
And thanks to new technology
The 'world's' our oyster now.
Computers, internet, and like,
Will simply 'spell out' how.

But, flowers, trees and birdsong,
Are the 'miracles' of life,
I can turn to their creator
To help me when there's strife.
A young child's 'happy laughter',
I will cherish all my days,
And human love and friendship
I will value *'that'* always.

So, let me ask for 'peace on Earth'
An end to 'futile war'.
The dawning of a 'brand new world',
Where *'fear'* shall reign *no more.*

Heather Overfield

RELIGIOUS PRAYERS, POEMS AND PROSES

Think of those

When you take a drink, think of those miserable persons and those poor creatures whose raging thirsts will never be quenched - *pray for them.*

When you eat, think of all the hungry grumbling stomachs in the world that will never be satisfied with fulfilling food - *pray for them.*

When you feel that you want to get away from all the worries of your little world, think of those who are dying and want to live on at all costs, and are so desperately holding on to life - yet, have nothing much in life to live for - *pray for them.*

When you feel rejected in love, think of those that have 'never known any kind of love', and *pray for them.*

When you frivolously exclaim: 'What a hope!', think of those with 'no hope', and *pray for them.*

When you are weary, think of those who are being tried 'beyond anything that you have ever had to endure', and *pray for them.*

When you are happy, think of the sad, and *pray for them.*

When you are in pleasant company, think of the lonely, and *pray for them.*

When you are feeling secure, think of those living in dire fear, and probably have been for much of their lives - *pray for them.*

When you are looking for a way, look to God; pray to Him, and ask Him to look beyond your own worries and to concentrate on the troubles of the world, and all the persons, and all the creatures 'much-less fortunate than oneself'. *Pray for them.*

Mary Pauline Winter

Prayer

I believe in prayer
Because I'm sure that it works.
It helps to relieve the suffering:
The mental and physical hurt.
The voice of prayer may be thistle-light,
Dissolving quickly in the air.
But it reaches Our Lord who is listening
Because He's here, there and everywhere.
No-one today has seen Him,
The Greatest Man on Earth,
Except Saints and those so blessed
With enormous spiritual worth.
There's so much more to the spoken prayer
Than aimless, repetitive words.
The heart must be behind them
And a soul that wants to be heard.
Prayer gives us faith and hope and courage
In a most unusual way
That's with us through the darkest night
And the stressful, drawn-out day.
There is a meaningful reason
We were born to live and finally die,
But we spend our lives forever asking,
Why and why, and why?
One day we'll know the answer
And then we shall come to see,
A Paradise home that is waiting
And why prayer is the eternal key.

Raymond Kirby

Heartfelt Orison

The sun dips sinking to its rest
When Lord I think of You,
And how You put me to the test
Every long day through.
And as the dark of night appears
I know how much You care,
For You have wiped away my tears
And I thank You in this prayer.

I think of flowers and the trees
They're so much part of You,
And in the buzzing of the bees
I hear life spring anew.
The sea, the sky and countryside
Where e'er Your Grace has been,
Within my heart will ever bide
This beauty I have seen.

And as I close my eyes in sleep
I hear the angels' choir,
Singing all Your praises deep
And lighting hope's great fire.
Then when the morning sun once more
Shines on this land so fair,
I'll thank You as I have before
In a fervent prayer.

Len Fox

MY BEDTIME

Mummy said, 'It's time for bed'.
So in bed I led.
'It's time for a story' she said.
Cuddled me in my duvet
I said, 'Hooray'.
It had been a long day
Still so many things to say
But tomorrow is another day.
She gave me a hug
And said, 'Cutch up snug'.
She kissed my cheek
Which she did every night of the week,
Close your eyes now and don't peek
It's time for sleep.
She said, 'I love you Honey'
I said, 'I love you too Mummy'
Goodnight
Sleep tight.

Cheremane Hartery

The Question And Answer Prayer

Why is it that so many people
Want to go after God,
When Satan gives them such
A hard time?

Isn't it all about
Enjoying God?
When He shines through
Adding a new dimension to Life!

Having faith to reach for the sky
Reaching out to the One who gives Hope!

The enjoyment of God is more than just a
Moment; it is
Minutes,
Hours,
Days spent in His Presence.

I want to pray for others!
Praying for them will build me up;
Encourage me to move forward,
Towards more love for God and the
People He has made.

Fears of stepping out in front of many.
Confidence will come from You.
Help me to go for it, God.

My self needs Prayer
It is difficult to love others.
Couldn't my friends turn out to be my enemies?

I need to get over this hurdle of learning to
Trust. Turn to God who is Light.
I will find protection and strength to
Face another day.

Eva Young

THANK YOU

I thank You Lord. I know You heard.
Every word.
Even those I never spoke.
Those I said asleep before I woke.
I know You can see,
The beauty inside me.
The good and the bad.
The happy and the sad.
I know You have me in a mould.
And as I fight, You firmly hold.
You shape and touch,
And show how much,
You really care.
You tease each hair.
All my hopes and desires.
Are what *Your* beauty inspires.
I thank You for letting me be.
Frail as I am, in Your eyes, full of dignity.

Dawn Rudderham-Thornhill

AM I A FOOL?

People think me such a fool
Because I follow God's golden rule,
They think that I am blind and cannot see
What life on this Earth is meant to be.

God to me is a shining light,
So I look to Him both day and night,
When I am wrong and I make a mistake
I ask for God's forgiveness before it is too late.

They think that my life it not much fun
But I am as happy as anyone under the sun,
For my life I devote to my family and my God
Until the day my body rests under the sod.

Jean-Ruth

THE TACTILE CHRIST

('He took her by the hand . . .' Mk 1:31)

Take me by the hand,
And raise me to my feet;
Aid me by your grace -
Bring victory from defeat.

Take me by the hand,
All evil thoughts expel.
Take me by the hand,
My unhappiness dispel.

Take me by the hand,
So others I may serve;
Take me by the hand,
So I'll not lose my nerve.

Take me by the hand,
And at the close of day
Let me see your face -
Be thyself the Way.

Maria-Christina

Poetic Prayers

Lord, give help and courage to those who ask of it
In Thy name.
Bless those who are in poor health
In Thy name.
Give comfort to those who are lonely
In Thy name.
Give riches to the poor
In Thy name.
Give food to the hungry
In Thy name.
Help us to have a greater understanding of Thy Word
So that Thy will be done.
Let us be humble in Thy sight
So that Thy will be done.
Help the world leaders with their decisions
So that Thy will be done.
Guide us in our decisions at all times
So that Thy will be done.

David Wynne

COPPICING

Clear out the dead wood,
make a path thro' the trees,
let some of God's sunlight filter in,
so the layers beneath feel the breeze.

Cut out the dead zones,
clear out waste from the soul,
let some of God's caring filter in,
so the inner spirit grows more whole.

Set by some quiet,
give an ear to God's speak,
let some of God's wisdom filter in,
so His Spirit's power we may seek.

'Lord, I am listening
in the depths of my soul,
I pray that Your message filters in
to renew, revive, make us whole.

Clear out the dead zones,
make a path thro' my heart
to let Your energy filter in,
so I effectively do my part:-

Share out Your message,
help awareness to grow -
we can let Your Kingdom filter in
by the *living* example we show.'

Ann Voaden

The Bible

Suddenly the silence of the library was broken,
As loud sounding words from a child were spoken,
'Daddy! Why is that old book with the others so new?
It looks so out of place, and should be removed.'

Arm round the child, the father patted her head,
'That book is not out of place dear Daughter,' he said,
'Just stop for a moment and take a good look,
Read of the miracles performed, in that dirty old book.

Read of a man sent from God, to show us the way,
To teach what is right, so that we should not stray,
From the path of temptation, evil and greed,
How to help other people, in their hour of need.

It tells of miracles performed by this man,
Healing of the sick, by the touch of His hand,
With five fish and just two loaves of bread,
Fed a multitude of people, who begged to be fed.

Christianity was then born, at a terrible cost,
For this man of God, was nailed to a cross,
Jesus was not a hero waving a sword,
A man preaching the gospel, words of the Lord.

Take this book home dear child, read it right through,
It reads like a fairy story, but believe me it's true,
The words in this book, will read as no other,
Learn from the words written, heed not the cover.'

Leonard J Negus

A Prayer For Comfort

You are near me in the morning,
And through the dark of night;
Though my spirit move from Heaven to hell
You bring eternal light.
        God is near, have no fear,
        For His love surrounds me.

My restless spirit wanders,
You know the path for me;
I only see through darkened glass,
My soul is yours to see.
        God is here, He is near,
        Love is all around me.

You hold my hand and see my faults,
Cast evil out from me;
That I may come close to Your heart
For all eternity.
        God is near, I am dear,
        With His love around me.

I thank you, Lord, for this my life,
You know my inmost heart;
And I will praise You all my days
Till I this life depart.
        God is here, His message clear,
        Love is all around me.

Anne James

FOLLOW LIFE'S PATH

I feel so young inside, as if time has stood still,
Yet I am so tired of giving, I question is life real?
Each day arrives, a new beginning, the future still lies ahead,
So many days when my heart rules, taken over by my head.
Life is precious, so much to learn, to share and this life to live,
Weary of excuses, explanations, exhausted by give, give, give.
A happy medium of living, loving, always learning and sharing,
Why oh why can't life be just this and accepted as caring?
There is so much throughout life that we continue to learn,
A wonderful gift is to listen, understand - show concern
To our own, to those we love, show them the path, the way,
Then left to each individual, to choose right from wrong not sway.
Life for everyone on this Earth however short or how long,
Should continue that path, always choose right, hopefully not wrong.
Follow that path of life that, may at times seem far too long,
Follow that path - all around nature gives to you and to you, belong.
Sometimes in life you question where to go, or what is the right way?
So easy to go wrong - sometimes so easy to sway.
Who knows how, or when life on Earth will end?
Till then believe, follow the Lord's word He will inevitably send.
Live life to the full, with love, sharing and happiness,
Strive always for strength, understanding, truth, never settle for less.
Always continue to follow the path of life and to give,
For whatever length of time, here on Earth we shall live.

Irene J Mooney

Dear Jesus

As I lay me down to sleep
I pray dear Lord You shall keep
My family safe and free from harm
Send me dreams to settle and calm
Bless this house by night and day
And childish fears please chase away
Heavenly Father hear my prayers
For I know You listen I know You're there
God bless Mummy, Daddy and Nanny Joyce
For in Your love we do rejoice
God bless my teacher and dear Mrs Clark
For they are always in my heart
So dear Jesus if I might
Ask a favour through prayer tonight
Stop all wars please make my world safe
I ask this prayer for all our sakes

Ann Hathaway

Reflection

I know dear Lord throughout this day
That from Thy path I've strayed
This morning's good intentions
I seem to have mislaid

Give me the strength in days to come
To try to make amend
And welcome You into my heart
My Saviour Lord and friend

Ian Russell

Show Me The Loving Way

Grant me O Lord upon this day
Your gracious love beyond all love
All good may I perceive this way
In purity as the dove

Enlighten good within my soul
Indifference allay
Humble my raging heart
Teach me heaven's way

Strengthen me when I pray
Install Your perfect sanctity
Wash away from me all fear today
Release me from vanity

Let no unholy thought remain
My will shall be my cross
Within Your shelter appertain
Never being ignominious

May my pilgrimage when complete
Lay my soul around Your door
Shall memories of love and life
Stay with me ever more.

Roger S Foster

SUCH A QUESTION!

I entered into prayer time
tears coursing down my face.
Lord, why do children suffer,
Why in this Earthly place?
Why do they have such sicknesses
from which some can never recover?
Why are some so badly used
in one way or another?
Why are some without a father,
for some a mother isn't there.
To some there's neither one of them
and no-one else to care.
No-one can tell a little one
the reason for the pain.
Oh Lord I need understanding
I don't look for who to blame.
I too was once a child,
back then I knew of pain.
I had no understanding
all I knew was shame.
Now when I see one hurting
my own starts up anew.
I want to draw them to me
not knowing what else to do . . .
Amen

Rosie Hues

Prayer For All, 2000

A quiet life and peace of mind,
Is what we need, so please be kind.
Problems solved, while we have slept,
Secrets safe, secure and kept.
For each and all, a prayer that's said,
While we lay, peacefully in bed.

Veronica Sharples

A Prayer

As I kneel by my bed to say my prayer
I forget all about my worry and care,
So too, life's problems, all that which I fear
When I talk to God, seem to disappear,
I kneel in reverence at the end of each day
Knowing full well, He hears what I say,
I ask for pardon for ways I have erred
He forgives and forgets, it says in His word,
My spirits are lifted as I start the new day
Having knelt by my bed my prayers to say
Praying a much better person to be
And thanking God for listening to me . . .

E M Wollen

Prayer Of Love

I pray that when you come to me,
That you will know that I am free,
You know that I will always be,
Waiting patiently for thee,
My prayers are answered I see,
Our love is deep, deep as the sea,
As long as I live, you! Will be,
The only love for me.

Barbara Scrivener

THANKS BUT NO THANKS!

Tears will not cleanse a broken spirit,
Despair devastates, plans become redundant, dreams put away.
Uselessness condemns, we make our own prison,
Questions without answers, another long perplexing day.

Cries are heard but grief clouds understanding,
Sympathy hurts, it's not what we need.
Impossible to convey this mental anguish,
Pride is bound in chains longing to be freed.

We live through pain alone,
Our mortal coil tightens, out fate is made secure,
Fear of loneliness sows seeds of hopelessness,
A vicious circle forms, we struggle to endure.

We are loved, we love in return but
Kind words are not easily accepted when depression reigns.
If one cannot help oneself how can others help?
Logic has no place, constant analysis strains.

A troubled mind inside a troubled body,
To love and be loved is life's greatest blessing,
To love when a burden is priceless but
Remorse overflows, we pass on our suffering.

How can one justify a family's selfless devotion?
This is not right, this is no way to live.
God please understand an invalid's cry,
I no longer want to take, I just want to give.

Frances Roberts

THANK YOU

As I clasp my hands to pray
And look back on my eventful day
And thank the Lord for all He's done
Taking care of everyone.
I hope tomorrow will be as bright,
Thank you Lord God bless, goodnight.

L M Kingsbury

THE MYSTIC OF TWILIGHT

Why does it seem that the twilight hour,
Is endowed with unusual and magical power,
Views which in daytime seemed drab and grey,
Now have an appearance, misty and fey.

Everything is shrouded with the coming of night,
Enfolding all in its mystic light.
Today life is hectic and full of stress
And in moments like this, one has to confess,

How pleasant to relax in this atmosphere of calm,
Absorbing nature's grandeur with all its charm,
A tonic to revive and strength to borrow,
To meet the problems we'll face tomorrow.

E Kathleen Jones

CHRISTMAS

What is there to say
That has not been said
Of the Holy Child
In His manger bed?
Of the animals, kneeling
To worship their King:
Of the angels, making the heavens ring?

Yet we in our time
Must find words to adore,
And if they have all
Been used before,
That does not matter
To you and me
As we join in the heavenly harmony.

E M Watkins

Poetic Prayers

When I go to bed at night
I pray to God to keep me right
Then I ask Him to look after my oldest child
And keep my youngest from the wild.

My church and congregation are next
That they be taught in the proper context
That the Bible be their book
And they are happy with the way they look.

Now it is time to say thanks to God,
For all his gifts especially good,
We must not always look for favours
But sometimes must show gratitude to our Saviour.

Beth McCracken

A Christmas Star

If we had followed the star like the wisemen
And taken gifts of gold
We would have seen Baby Jesus
And maybe this story told.

We would tell of the starlit stable
And of shepherds with their flocks
And steal a look at Jesus
In the manger, while Mary rocks.

We thank dear God for Christmas
And for that star up in the sky
We thank Him that we're here today
And sing His praises high.

Georgina Waite

My Millennium Prayer

What a tremendous end to the century
Clearing the Third World debt.
Giving poorer people a chance
For their meagre lives to enhance.
Proving the church, is such a powerful force
May everyone continue to endorse
Such hopefulness and trust.
For the Lord's followers is a must,
So give our God your best shot
For without His faith we are not
Complete, and not fully whole.
Please make us humble, in spirit and soul,
To be what you are, each day and night,
A beacon, encircled by your guiding light.

Norma Dawn Stewart

CONSOLATION

Here's a word of consolation
When your world has come apart.
Just keep on smiling, even though
It hides a broken heart.

We'll say a little prayer,
And think of you each day
To help you face with fortitude
Whatever comes your way.

To ease the pain you feel,
God helps you all he can
And if you've done your very best
He'll take and hold your hand.

Norma Pepper

Loves Lost

'We are here,' their spirits cry,
'We're standing near standing by,
Ever present ever near,
Watching o'er you shed a tear.'
Wishing arms could wrap around,
Giving love that is unbound,
They can hold you no longer,
But their love can't be stronger,
Though their bodies have gone away,
Their spirits will always stay,
Feel them near comfort to give,
Giving you the will to live,
God is there to hold your hand,
He knows it has all been planned,
Praise the Lord for those lost loves,
Look upon them as white doves,
Love from Him will ever flow,
To all above or below,
Give your love to Him on high,
Hold in your heart those who die.

Nicolette Thomas

GUIDE US DEAR LORD

Guide us dear Lord please guide us
Through all our daylight hours
Not just through sunshine's brightness
But dark and dismal showers.

Guide us dear Lord please guide us
Through all of life's harsh learning
That we may journey onwards
To find our hearts' true yearning.

Guide us dear Lord please guide us
Through each moment of the year
Help us to be more loving
By our overcoming fear.

Guide us dear Lord please guide us
Through the lessons of each day
And help us to remember
Your help best comes when we pray.

Tina Lipman

Ash Wednesday - A Penitential Psalm

O Lord, I'm sick to death of being me.
What happened to the me I should have been?
I wish I were different, the way you purposed me.

Sick of routine that entraps me,
Habits that enslave me,
Cage of circumstances, mostly self-created,
Network of misunderstanding, failure,
That weaves across my life.

Weary of feet so clogged in clay
Whilst forever I glimpse another way
Of being - far beyond my grasp.

Liberator, come to set the captive free,
Free me.

*'Do you repent of your sins?
Do you renounce evil?'*

Sometimes, when sufficiently aware of what that means.
I have become somewhat desensitised.

'Do you turn to Christ?'

I try, though sometimes I lose my sense of direction.

'Thou, art dust and unto dust thou shalt return.'

I know. I am aware of that.
So are other people dust, people I love.
I mind about it.

'Before the world was made, I chose you,
Chose you in Christ,
To live in love in my presence.'

Thank you. I need to remember that.
I'll keep trying then.

Help, please.
Don't give up on me.

Frances Lewis

A Blessing For Today

The blessing of God Almighty the father of all creation, of all things visible and unseen. The architect of our firmament and the giver of life both here and in the vast cosmos itself, be with us now both in our physical form and in the spirit world beyond.

May the love of Jesus Christ be also with us in our daily life, especially in our fellowship with one another. Through him and in his name may we find the path to perfect peace.

To the Son and the Father and the Holy Ghost be accorded all honour and majesty, and through the miracle of creation and the mystery of the crucifixion may we humbly strive to continue to live closer to thy holy will.

We ask this only to serve and expect nothing back in return, save for our daily bread and deliverance from evil transgressions. Guide us along the way of righteousness which is the path to eternal glory both here and in heaven.

Lastly, forgive us our sins and misdemeanours, strengthen and guide us in our daily lives, through the name of our dear Lord who lives and reigns with the Father Almighty for ever and ever.

Harry Lees

God Of All Things

God of all things;
harbinger of grace and beauty, of inspiration and creation,
flowing inside us like an eternal ocean at peace,
help us to understand finally
that finding the way back home is really possible,
that indeed we were always home but could not see it
through our forgetting minds.
Grant us the gift of knowing, of seeing with fresh eyes,
of true comprehension, that we too may light up the sky
with the love that we have uncovered afresh
on our journey back to you.

Carol Ross

Remember To Pray

Stretch out your hand dear Lord
And touch the weary soul
Comfort the sick and dying
And make their spirits whole.

So many people need your help
In this world today
Their living seems so pointless
As they stumble along the way.

The world is in a turmoil
Almost everyone at war
Some people losing everything
Feeling lost as never before.

If only they'd remember
To stop and say a prayer
When things seem really hopeless
God's love is always there.

Mary Lunn

A Daily Prayer

Thank you, dear Lord, for Your tender, loving care
And Your abundant gifts beyond compare.
With Your abiding Love which all transcends,
Please cherish all my family and friends
And to every lost and lonely soul
Send Your Holy Spirit to make them whole.
Dear Lord, please help me in every way
To do Your perfect bidding day by day,
Be at my side in all my daily life,
Help me to overcome the storms and strife.
Keep me calm and serene, O Lord, I pray,
Whenever in temptation's path I stray.
Give me the strength to help myself and then,
Grant me the power to help my fellow men
And when I finally come to You at last,
Please forgive my transgressions of the past.

Joan Weston

My Prayer

Good Lord in Heaven, hear my plea,
I won't ask you Lord to pity me,
But if my troubles become hard to bear,
Help my Jesus, to show that I still care.

Guide me Father in my life,
Love my children and my wife,
Bless the home that we have made,
And may angry words forever lie unsaid.

I ask this Lord in thy Holy Name,
Rebuke me Father, should I be vain,
Look down on us from high above,
And shower us with thy Eternal Love.

Ernest Rendall

For The Children

(For Alexandra Leigh and David James)

We take so much
We leave the future bare
For thy loved ones who we care
The land is raped, the loving is scarce
Torture, murder, creed and hate
We must all change before it's too late.

Can we resolve all the past?
Can we save the future?
Let there be a new peace and new love,
One sent down from God above
A pure fresh undying love.

Children of our future
Deserve a chance
Let them play and sing and dance
For they will save us all
And to all our ancestors
That have gone young and beautiful
Thank you for your wisdom and light,
You travel through the night
Looking for a New Saviour strong and right.

Amanda Woodhouse

A SILENT PRAYER

How often do we knee l and say,
Thank you Lord for another day.
For the love that you give us
And your blessings too
Where would we be
If it weren't for you?
You guide us in our work and play
Show us how to live life in the right way -
When we are worried, or we are sick
We pray that you will help us quick.
Never do we as pray, say,
'Hello Lord, how are you today?
With all the burdens of the world on you,
Is there anyway we can help you?'
Oh no! Selfish mortals are we all,
Yet, we expect you to hear us when we call.

Doreen Petherick Cox

A New Day

Heavenly Father, Creator of all living things,
I thank you Lord for what each day brings.
Joyous laughter, life long friends
Please help me to enjoy this day.
Sincerely doing of my best
To help all people who may be in distress.
Mother's with toddlers, who are so ill,
Please Lord help me with goodwill
To be always thankful for all I have.
For families who share so much together,
Be it good or bad.
Sick people everywhere need help my Lord,
Help me to understand it's not just people
Who live near to my doorstep.
But all people abroad.
The hungry, the dying all who suffer from
Leprosy, AIDS, those with loss of limbs.
The sinful who are full of remorse,
Put your hand on them Lord.
Help them to change their course.
People in Mozambique who are suffering from
Terrible floods and disease.
'A country in so much distress.'
Please dear Lord help me to do my best,
Let all aid come their way,
To relieve all the homeless, sick people
Who are very frightened folk.
Please make them feel dear Lord, you
Are close at hand.
I thank you for all priests who teach us to pray
Thank you my Lord for each new day.
Amen.

Betty Worley

New Life, New Hope

May your life be smooth and tranquil
From its dawning to its end
And to share your joys and cares
May you never lack a friend.

May you find your true vocation
May your destiny be clear
For uncertainty and doubts
Are what gives rise to fear.

May you see the beauty in the world
And simple pleasures find
May you know good health and happiness
And always peace of mind.

Mandy Smith

On The Wings Of Love

Love for sale,
That's what I felt like,
There was so much more,
More that I could give.

But I couldn't find them,
The wings of love,
To guide me over the cliff
And down to the valley.

But you slowly took hold
And lifted me up,
Out of the rut,
That had kept me still.

You show me new sights,
How mighty the lion is,
Within the little cub,
That was me.

Down the humble path,
I had found my strength,
But it wasn't really mine,
It belonged to the mighty lion.

Thank you for using me,
When I felt useless,
Help me to keep roaring
And not disappear in a whimper.

In weakness I am strong,
Though it's beyond comprehension,
I know it to be true
When I am there with you.

Melanie Mockler

Emily's Angel

Little sweetheart look up high
Can you see who's in the sky?
See that star that shines so bright
Grandma's come to say goodnight.

Now tucked up and fast asleep
A watchful eye Grandma will keep.
So sleep tight my precious love
An angel's watching from above.

Leslie Hogarth

A MORNING PRAYER

I will arise and lift my eyes,
As I come to the Lord in prayer,
I see, with joy, a morning star
And I know the Lord is there.

I ask the Lord for his gentle strength,
To journey through the day,
I ask the Lord for his inner peace
And to take my burdens away.

I ask the Lord to forgive my wrongs,
To correct my erring ways,
To keep me humble in all I do,
To serve Him, all my days.

I thank the Lord for his selfless love,
For giving his life for me,
For teaching me, through His Holy word,
For the truth, which sets me free.

Yes, I will arise and lift my eyes,
To a heaven, inside my mind,
Where all is sweet, and all is new
And the wind, is gentle, and kind.

E McGarry

Morning Offering

Eternal God, take my thoughts this day
And shape them to Thy will.
Creator God, touch my heart with grace.
Redeeming Christ, show me now Thy way
And lead me to Thy Holy hill
Where I may see Thy Godhead's face.

O Christ my Lord, let each word I say
Bring praise unto Thy Holy Name.
Son of God, form my words by day and night
And teach me how to pray.
Incarnate Word, guard my life from sin and shame
That I may see the glory of Thy light.

Holy Spirit, take each deed and thought
And make Thy home within me.
Kindle in my soul a flame this day;
Sanctify my life so dearly bought
Upon the Cross at Calvary
That I may rise above this mortal clay.

Uvedale Tristram

SUNDAY MORN AWAKENING

I awoke this very morning, and the sun was shining bright,
Its beams played on my duvet cover, in brilliant yellow and white,
Then I realised how lucky I was, that God had created for me
A glorious morning awakening, so bright for me to see.

I thanked Him then for waking me, from my slumber deep,
And all the dreams that came to me, whilst I was asleep,
But best of all his creation, around me everywhere,
That I could take within my eyes, by every blink and stare.

I looked out of the window, and saw his hand again,
Had painted the crocuses yellow, and detailed every vein,
Along with the snowdrops swaying, in the gentle breeze,
I wanted to capture this moment, with photo, so it would freeze.

Allowing me to remember, what God has done for me,
And all the glories around me, in form of flower and tree,
So thank you God for bringing, the sunshine and the rain,
That gently warms or wets, my special window-pane.

Nigel Lloyd Maltby

YOUR FINAL JOURNEY

Today you start your journey
To a new life far away.
It will be a happy one with
No sadness or pain to bear.

For those of us you leave behind
Your loved ones and friends,
It will be a sad time
When we all will shed tears.

But the memories we have of you
Will soon dry our eyes of tears
And once again we will smile
When we hear your name.

So farewell our dear one
Who has left us at an early age
Your life and love will always be with us
At every stage of our lives.

Farewell dear one.

Margaret Wood

FREEDOM FOR ALL

Holy One we love you
Sinners that we are
Jacob's Ladder is slippery
Have mercy on us
Help us step by step.
Keep our thoughts clear
No evil to see or hear
Hail Mary our blessed
Mother of Christ.
Lord God of Israel
Jesus the sign to guide us
It is written the gospels
To comfort and help us
The Blessed Word from
The Creator of all.
Holy Spirit may your
Ever flowing fountain of love
Cleanse us with joy and
Freedom from sinful ways,
Give us the wisdom from
The spirit that lights
Our universe for all Eternity.
Amen.

Duncan MacFarlane

Millennium Prayer

What are we expecting to happen
When the clocks strikes the end of '99?
Will there be earthquakes and eruptions?
Is God going to give us a sign?
To tell us to treat the next millennium
With more respect than we did the last.
To conserve God's living creatures
Not destroy them as in the past.
To live together in peace and love,
Respecting another's colour and creed,
To find ways to work together
And forget the cult of greed.
Two thousand years ago a Child was born
Whose life brought light from dark,
2000 lies ahead, an empty page,
Let His word make the first mark.

Joan Gray

I Love My Lord

I fear no man, no evil deed
I shall not weaken.
I cry no tears for the wicked heart
I seek not for what, I wish I had.

I Love my Lord.

I fear not the darkness
In the dead of night,
Though the curtain may be drawn
Before the morning light.

I Love my Lord.

I waste no dreams
On the fortune of wealth,
No growing desire
For perfection.

I fear not the passage of time
For I have travelled
The road of faith,
And rediscovered, everlasting grace.

I Love my Lord.

The light shone and glowed within
Lifting my soul, beyond sorrow's reach
Placing me in the hands
Of my keeper.

I Love my Lord.

B G Ryan

The Wonder Of You, Lord

Softly and gently the cool misty rain
Caresses my face, again and again,
Wild rhododendrons lying wind-blown and torn
Carpet the footpath that is narrow and worn.
A distant splash turns to thunderous roars
As down from the rock face a waterfall pours,
Cascading like satin, translucent and bright
Shattering the rock pool in an explosion of light.
Tall pines sway vigorously in a mid morning breeze
As I pass by, they bow low with an elegant ease.
The view from the hill top defies time and space
Clouds o'er the mountains drape like curtains of lace,
Invading the landscape shadows dance and creep
As the sun in the sky plays hide and seek.
A river meanders through the valley below
Where the call of a wood pigeon is hushed and low.
I climbed this hill Lord, to admire the view
But what I truly see, is the wonder of You.

Jean Mackenzie

A Cotswold Hymn

O God watch o'er your subjects,
Along the Cotswold way,
And help them to remember,
When working or at play,
You made those lovely Cotswold hills,
So peaceful and serene,
You made old Wychwood forest
And the meadow sward so green.

You made the Windrush river,
You made the Dikler brook,
You made the golden cornfield,
So man could build the stook
And as we would remember you,
Who gave His only Son,
Will you give us your blessing,
As through life's race we run?

Please bless the lonely shepherd,
With his sheep upon the hills,
The ploughman at the furrow,
As the Cotswold earth he tills,
The milkmaid in the dairy,
The stockman in the yard,
The carter at the horses head,
The poacher on his guard.

And as you give your blessing,
To each and every one,
Please help us to remember.
You gave your only Son,
Please help us to remember,
That you made the Cotswold dawn,
And with each mornings rising sun
All our joys will be re-born.

J E Sharpe

A Heaven

If there's a Heaven we'll surely meet again
A joy we can share forgetting the pain
To see you once more, to feel your embrace
Did you miss me at all?

Is there a smile on your face?
If there's a Heaven, I hope it will be
A haven of peace that will welcome me
With Mother and Father, Grandparents too.
All of my loved ones, there are quite a few.
If there's a Heaven I hope it will be
Such happiness there and a new life for me
I hope I will see, all the friends that once cared
From the days of my childhood.

In whose lives we once shared,
If there's a Heaven will the gates open wide?
But then, have I been good enough to be let inside
I hope I can say I've committed no sin
But am I quite worthy to be allowed in?

If there's a Heaven, how can I keep in touch
With all of my family? I'll miss them so much
I hope they won't mope, will get on with their lives
It's so hard as I know
But you can still survive
And if there's a Heaven
I hope at some time
All the people I love
Will be there that are mine.

M Pay

My Daily Prayer

Thank you Lord for another day
Thank you for helping me on my way
Thank you for all the good you do
Help me Lord to be like you.

Help me Lord to be good and kind
Help me remember to always find
The best in everyone, all around me
Help me to know, your love surrounds me.

I give you thanks Lord for my needs that are met
I know you have never failed me yet
I also pray I can enjoy good health
Which is more important than having wealth.

Thank you Lord for my loving family
And for all my friends,
For the love and support, I have from them
On which my life depends,
Thank you Lord for each new day
And for many more, I hope and pray.

Jean Wood

Thank You Lord

Dear Lord when I pray
Give me, is all I say
Forgetting all you do
For us each and every day.

Thank you, words so true
I don't say to you
I must count my blessings
For all the things you do.

Family, friends, I've got the lot
Never too cold or hot
Every day I must say
Thank you Lord for all I've got.

V Nelson

My Prayer Of Thanks

Dear Lord as I kneel before you
at the close of this day.
I thank you for all the love
You have shown to me today.

I thank you for the friends I have seen.
Your guidance has been evident in every
step I have taken.

Thank you for putting your arms around me to
comfort me. I felt them Lord. How I felt them.
They gave me the courage I needed to continue.

I have your love in my heart, and in my life.
What greater gift can I ask for?

I am alone as I pray. How strange I feel not alone.
The peace only You can give abides with me.
It takes away all the regret I feel, because I would
liked to have achieved more for You today.

I have seen your face shine on the faces
of the people I have met today.
I am remembering now the beauty I have seen on
the faces, and in the voices I have heard. People
who are struggling, and still managing to smile,
some in pain, and never complain.
Those who give, and never count the cost.

I have seen You in all of them today.
For this and all your gifts.
I give You my prayers of thanks Lord,
at the close of Your day.

Brenda Russell

A Millennium Prayer

A thousand years in the lifetime of man:
Reflect on the past and learn, if you can.
Our world is a treasure for all to share:
It will only survive if we learn to care.
A world full of wonders for all to enjoy:
A world which mankind has no right to destroy.
As guardians of all that the earth has to give
Let us pray we decide to let the world live.

Kathryn Strangeway

THE GIFT

Thank you God for this new day,
What a gift,
All wrapped up in the mists of dawn,
And tied with shining bows of morning.
I open this gift eagerly like an excited child,
And look inside,
It is filled with moments,
Minutes, hours, sunshine, showers,
Laughter and flowers,
Hopes and fears,
Joys and tears,
All these moments are mine
And I will cherish them everyone
And when they are gone,
I will open your new gift,
And that gift is called,
Tomorrow,
Thank you God.

A Heart

Dalesdown

Here I sit in the garden
Beneath the wind-whispering oaks;
The scents of summer grass are all around.
My eyes wander gratefully over tranquil fields
To distant hills. I will lift up my eyes to the hills
- soft in the noonday vale of mystery, gently marking
The horizon with their graceful curves, circling
For me a precious moment in time to be still
And to know that God is here.
Here, in the larks, whose tongues cut through
The air with silver scissors of sound, revealing
Intimations of the harmony that's yours - transcending
The intrusive bellow of the planes, roaring busily
To Barcelona, Budapest, Bosnia or Brussels;
These pass, but the larks remain.
Here, upon the wooded Sussex downs I may regain
My childhood innocence - the Christopher Robin days
Of wonder and enchantment with the world:
When cruelty and hate were unknown words.
Here in the garden and the fields your presence dwells
As much as in town churches
And office blocks and on the M25.
It dwells in the people that I see around me,
In the crow that steps unfearing on the lawn
Close to my feet; free to go or stay, silent and calm.
Oh Lord, I empty here my mind of shallow thoughts
And problems half-resolved.
I come to drink the cup of plenitude you offer me,
Which makes me new and helps me pray for others,
Refreshed with hope for the future.

Sylvia Herbert

ONLY A PRAYER AWAY

I spoke today to my Saviour, I do it every day
He's close by me at home and wherever I roam
He's only a prayer away.

If you're laden down with problems
And you find it hard to pray
Just do as I do, talk to Him too.
He's only a prayer away.

Tell Him your troubles and tell Him your joys
He listens, believe what I say
Pretty soon you'll begin, His presence to feel
He's only a prayer away.

One day we will all get to see Him
Praise be what a glorious day
Just how do I know that He loves me so,
He's only a prayer away.

As He folds His arms around me, how I long to hear Him say
I know how you tried, for there by your side,
I was only a prayer away.

Martha Mynott

A Carer's Prayer

O Lord please see me through
Each day and troubled night
For caring is a full time job
To which I give my life.

Lord give me strength and patience
Help me through each day
And when I'm tired and weary
Be with me as I pray.

Caring for a loved one
Takes all my strength away
But Lord with you beside me
I will manage through each day.

Sometimes when I am lonely
I put up a silent plea
That should I need a carer Lord
That you will care for me.

Hazel Wood

DIFFICULT TIMES

Life can be such a battle and I believe it's like that for you now
But you can and will get through it because God will show you how
I'm sure that you've come through before when you never
thought you could
So just keep going, because what you believe is true
And know that there are people around who are caring, and
praying for you.

Shirley Ann McGrath

THE STRAIGHT AND NARROW

Upon the straight and narrow path
        We pilgrims stand alone
And watch the opening of the gates
        That lead us to the throne.

Down here on earth our work is done
        With love and honour blessed
And now we're going up to Heaven
        For our eternal rest.

Safe in our Saviour's arms at last
        Our happiness assured
The strife is o'er
        The battle won
Peace now and ever more.

Leslie Thompson

MILLENNIUM PRAYER

God of the past, the present and the future
Hear now the praise and prayers we bring today
We find our world perplexing and confusing
We need your guiding light to show the way.

We come in weakness, conscious of our failings
Seeking the power which you alone can give
To conquer sins which seem to overwhelm us
We ask you now for strength to help us live.

Not for ourselves alone we ask your blessing
We think of those in trouble or despair
Victims of war and violent ways of living
Grant them your peace, O God, that is our prayer.

Two thousand years since Christ was in the stable
Bringing to us a God with human face
Why do we still ignore what we are offered?
Why do we not accept his love and grace?

God of the past, the present and the future
Help us to put our lives into your hand
So that we learn to live for one another
Bringing your love and care to every land.

Joanna Young

PRAYER FOR GUIDANCE

Lord of my happy days
Thee does my spirit praise
Be thou my guide
Think would I ever be
Lovingly joyfully
Use all thy gifts for thee
Be thou my guide.

In all life's history
In sorrow's mystery
Be thou my guide
Even in darkest night
Show me thy holy light
O mercy infinite
Be thou my guide.

Be thou my spirit's shield
My God, in Christ revealed
Be thou my guide
Worker of Galilee,
Lord of Gethsemane
Victor or Calvary
Be thou my guide.

Jo Rowan

PROGNOSTIC

As if the world was young
I see displayed
The snowdrop and the crocus in
The woodland glade
And where her suffrage to the
World is won
Even the little aconite aflame.

As if the world was old
The aspen dies
And clings to bine stems as her pulses sigh
Innate memorial to the passing sky
Only the barnless owlett stays.

As if the lustre and the world was wan
As if the mystery of the world has failed.

Hugh Twose

My Prayer

It really costs nothing, nowadays
To show someone you care.
Picture just about anyone,
And imagine yourself there!
If all the *haves* and *have-nots*
Decided once, to share,
Poverty and greediness, all
Would end just then and there!
Even infirm and able, could
Trade what they can do.
The first can sit, and watch, and hear
The latter, walk, and fetch, just do!

Pat Rapley

Prayer Of Trust

The worries - the danger
Breaking through,
May sometimes
Turn my heart to you.

The sudden panic in the night,
Where pulse quickens,
And heart takes flight;
May be your call O God most high
To reach out for your help, and cry.

For means to reach us
You know best,
In busy moments;
Or lives at rest
All we know and this hold dear,
That in extremes you are near.

Emmaus road,
Small boat at sea,
Your presence beckons
There for me.
Hold me firm
And give me strength
And time to thank
You Lord, at length.

Martin Winbolt-Lewis

AN EVENING PRAYER

Dear Heavenly Father, who lives above,
Protect my family, through this night.
Give us your peace, with perfect love,
To rest with Jesus, your true delight.

We thank you Father, for that new day,
When you sent your Son, to die for me.
In Jesu's holy name, we all must pray,
For He is the Lord, who died for thee.

Thank you Father, for your Holy Ghost,
Who was sent to help us, in each task.
I thank you Holy Spirit, we love most,
For He helps to do, everything we ask.

Give me thy strength, and your wisdom,
To live with Jesus, one day at a time.
Give me love, to live in your kingdom,
Where Jesus reigns, without any crime.

Forgive me dear Jesus, if I sin again,
Or do not forgive, any of my brethren.
Jesus who took my suffering and pain,
Is my Saviour, who leads us to Heaven.

Bless and keep safe, all our families,
Through each dark night and each day.
Give us joy in Him, who tells no lies,
So that God will answer, when we pray.

F Schofield

A Prayer To God

Each night in bed I humbly pray
For God to keep our sins at bay
With wars and crimes around the land
It seems Christianity is out of hand.

Has our Lord's message been all in vain
Is Satan at the helm again
God spoke of love which we must share
This is the answer to all out prayers.

It is up to us to heed his lesson
For neighbourliness is such a blessing
To leave out God is a grave mistake
We must follow him for all our sakes.

This is the answer there's no denying
We must keep the Christian banners flying
Let the whole world know God's Christian word
To miss this out is being absurd.

Lachlan Taylor

Wake Up Call

My world, wake up, hear me
Tis I your God praying now
I pray to *you* as a last resort
Your head is refusing to bow.

For decades now you have slept
Lived unhearing to myself
Leaving entirely alone all good values
Gathering dust upon your shelf.

I should not be in such
Situation now as to
I be praying to *you* at this time
I should be saying - 'How dare you?'

Instead I am on my knees
In one last effort I pray
Are you not shamed you have done this
All selfish to have your own way.

You have all now forced me
To carry the cross as my Son
You putting *me* on life sentence
And all other wrongs you have done.

You know that never did I
Allow abuse of Hallowed ground
For this was what my world once was
I pray to you on ultra-sound.

This is your wake up call
Please awake me in return
Awake me from my sorrow and sadness
And from my long time yearn.

Barbara Sherlow

The Lost Sheep

Of our sins there are so many,
but, of faith there is not any.

How can we now all be raised,
until your holy name is praised?

Some have let you be their guide,
others have stayed full of pride.

Outside your fold they all just seek to strive,
like machine slaves not knowing they're alive.

Scattered flock have now began to stray
and some have wandered far too far away.

Blessed are the ones who tried to make,
life better for the people and your sake.

Jean Paisley

If Death Comes

I do try hard Lord to do what I should,
And have to say, I am not always good.
Prayers said only occasionally,
Or when someone else prompts lazy old me.
Of course you're aware that I'm not quite old,
Reached an age, where I do just as I'm told.
At another day's end, I have no doubt,
If death comes for me, on you I can count.

S Mullinger

Where There Is Spirit

Our Father knows what's best for us
So why should we complain
We always want the sunshine
What complex lies in these few words
Blessed are the poor in spirit
And knowing God's love is unfailing.

His mercy unending and great giver of life
Is holding our hand and safe in his care
There is no need for seeing for in him we live
The mystery of life with all of its struggles, suffering and strife
What living things are words and language
How frequently they change their shades of morning.

But the life of the spirit
Is not restricted to holy places
Worship and spirituality is not confined
To Churches, Chapels and Monasteries
The spirit lives in people
There is spirituality in a smile in generous words.

There is no thinking person
Who can stand untouched today
And view the world around us
With the knowledge of your presence
May be guided by your spirit and truth
For there is no night without dawning and I know
that my morning is new.

Heather Aspinall

Thanks To The Lord

Before I close my weary eyes
I kneel down and pray
To thank the Lord for everything
He's given me that day
I ask him to look after
Every animal, plant and tree
The hungry, homeless, men at war
Even my enemy
I pray He will look after
Every one of us. His sheep
Then I gently shut my eyes
And peacefully go to sleep.

Carl Fricker

Just Let Me Listen

Lord, at the end of this busy day
As usual there's lots I would wish to say
But just for tonight let me be quiet and still
And listen, that I may obey your will.
Let my mind become open to you
Responding to what you want me to do.
And as weary under the covers I hide
Please come to me and lay by my side.
Protect and comfort me as I sleep
Waking me in the morn from my slumber's deep.

Sue Goodman

PRAYER

A prayer from the nation,
Lord I plead through your Son,
Seeking your blessing,
For weary travellers, each one,
As you survey your kingdom
And observe the poor in the land,
Feed their needs and their spirits
By your servants' hands,
A prayer for the crown,
That their hope rests in you
And they discern your will
In all that they do,
A prayer for the family,
Closer than the state and great kings,
That you bless them and keep them
In the shade of your wings,
A prayer for your child,
As I approach that Heavenly place,
To intercede for my fellowman
Before the King's throne of grace.

Patricia Thompson

Penitential Psalm

Great Maker of the sky and earth,
dear Mother God, whose love gave birth
to rivers, oceans, mountains, trees,
where creatures all might live in peace.

Each living creature great and small,
You set us humans over all
to be the image of your grace
and rule as regents in your place.

Forgive our sin of deadly pride
which from the first your law defied,
and poisoned all posterity
with fruit of the forbidden tree.

For, though You gave your only Son
to die for love, and make us one
with You, our Maker and our Friend,
a broken world to heal and mend,

Still must we exercise our power
to kill and maim both beast and flower,
in place of love sow seeds of hate
and your creation desecrate?

O, turn to flesh our hearts of stone!
Send down your Spirit, Holy One,
that we may do your will on Earth,
true to that love which gave us birth.

Joan Sheridan Smith

THANK YOU FOR THESE WORDS

The answers are here for us to find, and I know they lie deep
within our minds.
Truth is above all what we seek, and truth I pray for these words
to speak.
I pray to God and spirits around, to guide these words so that
peace can be found.
I know you listen, I feel you near,
as, 'Our journey to God' it starts right here . . . Amen.

Vicki Michele Loveday

Poetic Prayers

Our Lord give me this day,
Help and Guidance for me to pray.
Please help others worse off than me,
This I pray while on bended knee.
This prayer is to cure all my ills,
Because I'm taking so many pills.
If this You could do for me,
Then it will be my final plea.

Amen

Patricia Marples

CHRIST CRUCIFIED

He died - didn't He!
Just for you and me
He died - didn't He!
Excruciatingly for all to see
He was spat upon
He was thrashed and beaten
To a bloody mess
Just for you and me.
What was it all for?
'God's will,' He said,
'For the forgiveness of all your sins'
A crown of thorns pressed onto His Holy head
And the blood trickled down His face
Then the cross -
Their dreaded cross of shame and torture,
Bang - the nails were hammered into His gentle hands,
Bang - the nails were hammered into His lovely feet.
A sword thrust into His Holy side
A last breath
Then - He died,
Just for you and me
A horrific and humiliating death.
Just for you and me!
God's will was done,
Then a miracle happened,
When all thought all was lost
There He was radiant and alive -
By His tomb
For all to see.
Jesus! Resurrected!
Just for you and me.

Margaret Smith

Morning Prayer

Holy Jesus, heavenly King,
My rock in all the storms of life
To thee my morning praise I bring
With thanks for love and peace of mind.

Almighty God of all creation
Ruler of the heavenly host
Our only hope of true salvation
Be near us when we need thee most.

Morning stars and crescent moon
Proclaim thy glory in the sky -
God of true unfurling love
Whose care will never pass us by.

Holy Christ I kneel before thee-
In distress my Lord was near,
He guides me on the untrod way
With Him beside there is no fear.

Marcella Pellow

WATCHING IN THE NIGHT

Watching in the night,
Waiting in the stillness,
Listening for your gentle voice,
The voice I know so well.

Watching in the night,
Waiting in the quietness,
Knowing you will listen
To all I have to tell.

Watching in the night,
Waiting for tomorrow,
Only you can see the future
Of my chosen way.

Watching in the night,
Waiting for the morning,
When everything that went before
Has gone with yesterday.

Watching in the night,
Looking to the future,
Waiting in the stillness
As the precious hours pass by.

Watching in the night,
Looking to forever,
Waiting for the freedom
When at last my soul can fly!

Barbara Manning

At The Beginning Of A Scripture Prayer Group Gathering

Heavenly Father,

May we always bear fruit in our love
for you and for each other.
At the final harvest may we be gathered
in to your heavenly vineyard
to remain with you for ever.

We ask this under the guidance of the Holy Spirit and through the intercession of your Son, our Saviour, Jesus Christ.

Martha Fear

A Prayer

Lord you are my ocean
You toss me with the tug of your tides.
Your stormy strength overpowers me.
Your blue-green vista
Opens my heart to eternity.

Lord I am the cliff you undermine
Till it falls in a tumble of groaning rock.
I am the sandbar you build, grain by grain,
to enclose the lagoon in peaceful water.
I am the coral building living beauty
In the calm of your tropic sea.

Lord you are my ocean.
In summer calm, encircling, enfolding me.
You are my ocean in winter's bitter storms.
Ending my wanderings in providential wreck;
Bringing me home in your swift current
To the harbour of your loving,
The harbour of your heart.

Lord I am a fish in your ocean
Buoyant in you, my element;
Finding there all I need.
Breath and food and motion,
Sustained, at ease, at home.
In you my life, my all.

Sister Elizabeth Grantham

God Bless You

May God bless you and keep you
In His tender care,
And His angels surround you
This is my prayer.
May the sweet love of Jesus
Enfold you each day
To guard you and keep you
As you go on your way.

May the love of our Saviour
Shine from your face,
As you take His love
Into every dark place,
And His richest gifts
Be bestowed upon you,
To help you and guide you
In all that you do.

May you keep close to Jesus
Take hold of His hand,
And though you may fall,
The Lord understands.
Whatever befalls you
He'll be by your side
Forever to comfort
To heal and to guide.

P Ravenscroft

THANK YOU

'Someone has to do it,' she said
When I enquired what she was doing at Christmas
She was right
For like hundreds of others
She was going to spend her time working in the local hospital
We all benefit from the selfless work of others
Who let us travel, eat and be safe
Those who look after us when we are sick
Those who care for the homeless
We thank thee Lord for those who love
And for those who care
Often hiding their own pain and loneliness
By making sure that others feel wanted and loved
Give them Lord your special peace.

Pat Allington Smith

Oh Lord

Please hear me, when I pray,
As I begin another day.

The birds, their early chorus sing
And milkman's bottles happily ting.

I pray for peace, upon God's earth
And everyone to show their worth
By helping others, when they can
To be a friend to every man.

No colour and no different race
To put a smile on every face
With arms outstretched
When things go wrong
To comfort, help, and make them strong.

'Oh Lord, please help,
I know you can
You are our Saviour
And once a man.'

Hazel McNeil Newman

MORNING PRAYER

Dear Lord I pray this morning, for the beauty of your day
And hope that you will be with me, the same as yesterday,
Just hold me with your guiding hand, and lead me where you will
If I should stray forgive me Lord and shelter me from ill.

Dear Lord I pray to thank you, for the love you give to me
And ask for grace that I may learn to love my enemy.
I beg you Lord to call my name if from your love I hide
And grant me when this day is through
Your blessing and your peace at eventide.

Barbara Scriven

Remind Me

Did I give a cheerful greeting
and was there brightness in my tone,
as there should be when two people are meeting,
or did I just utter a groan.

Did I show interest and listen to what someone had to say,
and did I give sympathy to their problem,
did I respond in a positive way
or did I just try to ignore them?

Did I remember to say thank you,
to someone who was thoughtful and kind,
and did I show gratitude as I should do,
or did I say nothing expecting them not to mind?

Help me to remember the things that please,
a helpful gesture or kind word,
done naturally or said with ease,
remind me,
kindness is never unnoticed or unheard.

Heather Pfander

PRAISE

Live Thou in me O God and fill my soul with praise
Mould me to do Your will, help me to walk Your ways;
Let me be strong in faith, my mind and body fill
With Your desire and power, that I may do Your will
Let Your love through me flow to friends who may forsake me
Give me patience, Lord, with those who irritate me
Fill my whole being with your love divine
That it may strengthen and control this feeble love of mine
O Father let me praise you still when troubles I must bear
And in the darkness find your presence ever there
Uphold me when troubled Lord, give me power in pain
When I fall into despair raise me up again.
O Father, Son and Holy Ghost to You my song I raise
Whate'er betide, You're by my side
And always hear my praise.

Barbara Saum

Forget About Me

Her infant gazed up from the straw
with small hands weakly curled.
She never dreamed this furtive birth
would one day rock the world.

Although her young son heeded first
the Voice within his head,
he did his share of chores at home
and learnt his father's trade.

But greatly did his mother fret
and scold him when he said
that he was not the son of Joe
He was the Son of God.

Then Mary's falling tears foretold
her own most bitter loss,
for on her heart that instant fell
the shadow of the Cross.

As he died, they heard him pray
that men might be forgiven,
and in that moment of deep shame
they *knew* there was a Heaven.

But still today the shadows are as dark
and mothers weep in vain.
The Innocents of Bethlehem
in Dunblane die again.

To pray for my own soul would seem
like selfishness indeed.
So please forget about *me* Lord
and save the world instead.

Ursula Kiernan

SEE ME

I watch you while you say your prayers,
I watch you while you weep,
I keep my vigil at your side
Until you fall asleep.
And then you dream of what I was
And what I've come to be
And I guide your sleepy eyes to find
The truth you cannot see.
I am the wind, I am the breeze
That ruffles through your hair,
I am the touch you always feel
Yet never know is there.
I am the sun that warms your face
And tilts your lips to smile
And all this time you thought I'd gone
I've been here all the while.
And as you wake I see the tears
Start coursing down anew,
But I know you weep with happiness,
For I've shown myself to you.

Andrea Kiernan

PRAYER

O God of our fathers, be with us always
Watch over thy children by night and by day
Guide us and keep us - make thou our stay
O God of our fathers, be with us always.

Thy hand that had guided thy servants of old
Thy strength and thy love in beauty behold
When our steps they may falter and see not the way
O God of our fathers, be with us always.

Give peace to all nations where there is strife
Open men's mind to a far greater life
We dearly beseech thee and humbly pray
O God of our fathers, be with us always.

Mary Livingstone

JESUS IS HIS NAME

Come listen to the stories of old, from times
gone by of how one man suffered and died, on
cold cruel nails, He was pinned, for all on
this earth hated Him,
Jesus is his name.

Yet from that cruel wooden beam, a ray of light
shone forth, from the Heavens above, then came
proof of the father's love, a loving heart to
prove, that yet He still loved us all
Jesus is his name.

Now we must learn to share His sorrow, heal His
broken heart, help Him over these cruel things
of the past, put right for what went wrong, for
what all people did then, our conscious must take
the blame, let Him to know we want His trust again,
Let him know how sorry we are for what was done to
Him, help Him over that cruel past. We must admit
in our hearts, that old wooden cross bore the prince
of Heaven.
Jesus is his name.

Jesus is his name, Jesus is his name, He died
to show how much He loved us, Jesus is His name.
He put us to shame, Jesus is His name, no courage
on earth do we have, Jesus shows us the way, yes
Jesus is his name.

Janet Middleton

My Prayer

Dear Lord hear the words I say,
As I talk to you, at the end of day,
Help me be a special man,
To follow in your worldly plan,
Make me realise the worth,
Of being here upon this Earth,
So I may help some other soul,
To struggle up and reach its goal,
Give me strength to carry on,
Along the path where Jesus shone,
And good health through my golden years,
To travel on, no worried cares,
Help me, help others, all my days,
Teach me all your special ways,
That, one day, when my life is through,
I can come and live with you.

Charlie Boy Smith

The Hand

I bought an egg cup once, because
I like the whiteness of it
And the way a hand moulded
Around its shape. Friends looked,
Admired, and thought, 'She must like
Egg cups.' And now I must have
Hundreds, marching round the walls:
Animal shapes and clowns
And some with names of towns,
And one, Limoges, dark blue and gold,
And some from Canada
That look like marble.
Pottery, porcelain, plastic
And even glass and wood;
Art deco, cups that once held
Easter eggs; and some that hold
Two eggs at once.

And I despair

Of cleaning them,
Or even counting them.

And all I wanted was the hand.
Hand clasping cup - like the hand
That clasps the cup that holds
The metamorphosed blood
Of one whose resurrection's
Often celebrated
By gifts of Easter eggs.
Sometimes in cups,
Sometimes with sculpted hands.

Dorothy Davis-Sellick

Unite Us, Lord

Lord, are we to grow planted alone,
singly, one by one in isolation?
Through our behaviour attention drawing,
by the sin in us relationships soiling.

Lord, may we be as flowers in a field,
rich in colour, gregarious and free.
Our peace, hope and joy to share,
your glory ever-seeking, praying and care.

Lord, may we learn to bear one another, to blend,
to live together as one, united in life's garden.
Lord, help us to want to live Your way,
to trust, worship and give You due praise.

Karen Wills

IMMACULATE

The shadow of mankind lengthens
Guilt dumped in the night
For everyone to stoop over.

Wheat tears that ground
A hundred fold with a slight no,
A timid yes will grasp the faith,

But few delight in harvests
Borne by Another's obedience
And immaculate countenance.

Marylène Walker

THANK YOU

Thank You for the wren
Still seen
For the goldfinch feasting
On seeds of fragrant lavender
Thank You for the reward
Of early morning rising
Seen in the first blush
Of dawn upon the land.
Thank You for these treasures
That money cannot buy.

The sparkling diamond droplets
After rain
And Your bow across the sky.
Thank You for the storm clouds
Each with a silver lining.
For Your painted sunsets
Over panoramic skies.
Thank You Lord for eyes to see
And minds to understand
The beauty of Your handiwork
The vastness of Your plan.

Helen Sharpe

Thank You For My Day

Dear Lord thank you for my joyful day,
And all your help along the way.
Thank you for showing me what I must do,
And help me to remember I'll always be guided by you.

Please may I always have strong faith,
And strengthen the little that I have.
So that I may ever keep,
A smiling face when I wake from sleep.

May I always be ready to help,
Another soul - should they yelp.
Not forgetting that come what may,
Mixing with others they will have a brighter day.

Thank you for giving me a nice clean bed,
Where I can safely lie my head.
For loving people all around,
Who help me over the most slippery ground.

Betty Green

MY PRAYER

Draw me to your side, Lord,
Take me by the hand.
Show me how to trust you,
Let me understand
That you alone can guide me
Through the perils of each day,
You alone can help me
When my footsteps start to stray.

Watch over my family,
Keep them free from harm
And when the night is falling
Make them safe and warm,
Give them love and friendship
And bring us all at last
Home to you forever
When our earthly days are past.

Valerie Sutton

Silent Lamb

Lamb of lambs
May I find mercy in your eyes
Father of all fathers
May I find mercy in your eyes
Creator of all creation
May I find mercy in your eyes
Beloved of the beloved
May I find mercy in your eyes
Healer of all healers
May I find mercy in your eyes
King of all kings
May I find mercy in your eyes
Light of every flicking candle
May I find mercy in your eyes.

D Grimwade

Entreaties

Show mercy to Thy children, Lord; not one of us is perfect.
Have patience with the wayward ones and guide them safely home.

Look kindly on the disabled, Lord, and support their determination.
For those who are tied to their beds, O Lord; help to ease their
natural frustration.

Take pity on the weak, O Lord; give them strength to carry on.
Unravel the threads in tortured minds, giving peace and tranquillity.

Remember the sick and dying, Lord; forgive all those who repent.
The distressed and distraught need Thy help, O Lord; grant them
Thy calm understanding.

Receive unto Thyself, O Lord, the souls of our dear departed.
Enfold in Thy loving arms, O Lord, all those who are broken-hearted.

Those without food, without homes, without clothes, all need
to be reassured.
To know You are with them, whatever their plight, to provide for
their earthly needs.

Accept our simple, earthly gifts, any service we can render
To You and Your children throughout the world; and in this way
Your love engender.

Doris McCartney

Dream On

As I lay my weary head on this soft white pillow
Lord take my thought and dreams and desires
And hold them for me for the morrow

Guard my sleep, oh great Jehovah
Give me rest and peace I pray
That on the morn I might awake
And be ready, fresh and willing to face another day

Through those wee small hours
The ones the clock ticks silently by
Let me lying there in the dark
Be moulded into the object of your power

Lord caress and shape my dreaming sleep
Give me fruitful plans to keep
Let your talent be at work in me
Showing through my time awake
Plans and schemes to profit and glorify thee

Colin Rixen

Let There Be God

'Let there be God!' I said,
    'For without Him
        our lives are void.'
'Let there be life!' said God,
    'That man may breathe
        and share my life.'
'Let us live free!' I said;
    and through His laws
        I found life free.
'This life is good!' I cried;
    and boldly took His hand in mine.
'Go, tell the world!' He said,
    'That it may see -
        full life is bound to Me.'

Felicity Plumbley

PRAYER

I kneel before Thee Father dear
And lift my heart and mind to Thee,
I know you'll dry my every tear
And ope' my eyes that I may see.

In Thee dear Lord I know I'll find
The answers to my every need,
Such peace, tranquillity of mind
Help me dear Lord thy words to heed.

Now Father dear, this boon I ask
As through your world I walk each day
Please guide me in my daily task
And grant me, always, time to pray.

Chris Lawery

Of Faith

I needn't search for words to say to you
What you already know.
Before I scarcely speak you hear
O hearer of prayer, search through
Me please for any painful way
That could, despite my uttered wants, tear
Us apart. How many eloquent psalms can say
What I am longing for much better,
Breathed by you, knowing the day
When others such as I, had need to pray?
And they'll be answered too!
You cannot lie, O greatest one.
Such yearnings *you* instilled you will see through.

Diane Burrow

MILLENNIUM CELEBRATION

Let us not forget
what the real and only
millennium means . . .

It must remind us
to celebrate the Holy Birth
of Christ our Sacred Redeemer
two thousand years ago
who suffered a dreadful death
upon the Roman cross,

to save mankind from
the evils of a turbulent world
and to teach us to care
and have concern
for all humanity
and guide us towards
the pathway to divine infinity . . .

Stephen Gyles

A Miracle

Miracles do work for those who believe.
But do not expect instant cures to relieve
Depression, anxiety, illness or long felt stress.
But trust God to make the pain less and less.

That is the secret to restore your health.
God plans each week with wisdom and stealth,
Guiding your day with actions to see, learn and receive
Awaking experiences that teach the mind to perceive.

To work miracles God gives you the power within,
The chance to heal yourself, if you want to win
The greatest struggle of your life to find the real you,
To uncover the hidden self, this is what you must do.

It may take months of whatever God sends,
Treatments, reading, accepting, trusting loving friends,
Accepting too days of misery, hurt, grief, even great pain.
If fears, loneliness, the darkness inside are really to be slain

Little by little, the miracle commences its work,
As lightness increases, vision clears beyond the murk.
Joy, peace, calm, contentment all begin to start
Filling you with healing, restoring love in your heart.

Yes, God can work miracles every day.
If you want to see them all you do is pray
That He will guide and love you all the way.
So peace in your heart will come and come to stay.

Esmé E Wilson

Overrule And Underline

Lord of the e-mail, the fax and the pager
Enter now and delete all that's not major
The calls on my life ever faster and faster
Save me O Lord from overload disaster
Give me a database of passwords and peace
With a spreadsheet before me may mouse control increase
And connect me most surely with life ever after.

Robin E Wood

My Prayer To Lord Jesus

Your heart is broken Lord Jesus many times
Each day you watch between the lines
To give us strength to willingly survive
Lord Jesus thank you for my pleasant life

No matter what our sinful lives bring
We look forward to your heavenly springs
Our sins you have already forgiven
Yet, we drive you to make a mournful decision

Forgive us Lord Jesus for all sin we do
What sorrow we bring to you
Every day of our lives we bring you to tears
We do not deserve any praise we intolerable miserable dears

You listen Lord Jesus to our tales of woe
We sinners do, here below
Your loving heart turns not away
But helps us to keep sin at bay

Your potter's mouldings are sadly ignored
No wonder you feel like being daily bored
With sinners full of self importance
We break your heart when you watch; always, at a full glance

Leave us to sink to the bottom of the pit
Where we deserve to be each day
A bit of punishment we ought to receive
It will make us surely eager to believe

Earthquakes, hurricanes and floods come regularly now
We should get down on our knees and bow
Fervently ask total forgiveness
And make you at last know human kindness

May my prayer give you joy and dry your tears
Lord Jesus come to live with your sinful dears

Alma Montgomery Frank

Millennium Reflection

With the passing of time let's not forget
That our dear Lord came to save all
Two thousand years gone the Lord still lives on
To love and to bless and to rule

So celebrate this *millennium* time
With the faith that *Jesus* does reign
His promise still holds as it did long ago
And His *holy spirit* remains.

May God bless you in the new millennium.

Adrienne Elizabeth Wingrove

The Pain

It hurts that pain
I wish that roaring pain
Would go away
I cry in pain

I hope it will go when I sleep lying in the bed

The flag that's flying in the sky
Is fluttering freely in the sky
Then I wake

The pain
That roaring pain
I hope it will go away very soon

It would be wonderful to be in no pain

Paul Lunnon

To My Guardian Spirit

I am remembering all of the others who have
gone into the light.

Thank you for guiding me back from the
light.
The right way, I think. I wish you
could do a miracle.

Thank you for the world.

Look after my father, John Robert - he is all I have left.

My Mam, her sister, and her mother have all
fallen with cancer and gone to join you.

They are the sunlight now.

Barry Welburn

A Prayer For All The World

My prayer is for the children,
Please keep them safe from harm.

Also for the elderly.
Please guide them by the arm.

Keep animals and insects
And all God's creatures safe and well,

The world is such a precious place,
Don't sound the old death knell.

Man has dealt it such a blow,
Please make us change our ways

Allow us to redeem ourselves
And live in goodness all our days.

J A Prescott

FAITH

There are times, in a quiet moment
As the evening shadows fall
And the stars look down, when I ask myself
Why am I here at all?
And I wonder where I am going -
How the rest of my life will be;
What is it that makes me the person I am -
Who, exactly . . . is me?
I feel certain our lives have a purpose,
I believe we are part of a plan,
I take comfort and hope in endeavouring
To do all I possibly can.
Perhaps there will be, in the future
A task, I alone, can do
That is vital to something - or someone,
Before my life shall be through.
I may never know the answers
But what matter, as long as I stand
Firm, in believing I'm needed,
And guided by God's loving hand.

Elizabeth Amy Johns

PRAYER OF THANKSGIVING

*(Jesus Said: 'Thy Faith Has Made Thee Whole -
Go In Peace' Luke 8: 45-48)*

Jesus you saved me when all else had failed me,
you held me and fears fell away,
Jesus you taught me my burdens you would carry,
your strength is my stay day by day.
Now as I travel on life's rough hewn pathway
I know you are there my by side,
to lead me, to guide me, oft times to chide me,
in you all my needs will be supplied.
So thank you Lord Jesus for lifting and loving me
and thank you for your pardon and grace
and thank you for the new life that now flows through me
because I know that you died in my place.

D E Buckman

White Linen

Who is she, in white linen
From purest flax made
Who leads us in worship
On her heart God's word laid?

Who gives of herself
As she ministers duly
The message of Jesus
And service done truly.

Who, when just a girl,
Felt God's holy call
To serve him as Christian
To help one and all.

Whose role is as 'servant'
As any priest's should
Whose teaching reflects, that
Christ be understood.

Whose love to God's people
Is shown in her serving;
Time given, unstinting,
And we undeserving.

Who, drawn from among us,
Her ministry sharing
In example, extending
Concern, love, and caring.

By Christ's own example
She longs to be known
In love to her neighbour
But, not stand alone.

God, then, in our sharing
Will stand at her side
And affirm her Priesthood,
Be it ever denied.

Jo Allen

JIM

Too much life to slip away
like you did!
Why didn't you share,
why didn't you say?

You spent too much time,
concern, on others!
You could have hinted
about your own bothers!

But then, that's not you -
you show an open hand
of friendship,
not a trip to your problem-land.

I missed your goodbye -
you would have enjoyed a good laugh!
You lived life to the max,
never believed in cocked-half!

I do not care if this merits a Booker,
I bet you're stuffing them up there at snooker!

Perry McDaid

A Prayer For All

A prayer for you
A prayer for me
A prayer for all
Whoever you be

Trust in the Lord
In heaven above
Give him your faith
And he'll give you his love

Believe in life after death
It is free from all pain
Have truth in your heart
And be reborn again.

S A Ward

Take My Hand

Jesus take my hand on this lonely road
Earth has turned to sand, my heart a heavy load
Lift up my head lest roses see a teardrop fall
Let my eyes feel sunshine, help me to walk tall

Jesus as I speak your name silently in prayer
A rainbow fills the heavens, you are everywhere
Sending signs of love, the whole world is my friend
Songbirds' sweet music to my ears doth lend

Jesus bless soft breezes kissing tearstained eyes
Butterflies who comfort me playing in the skies
Flowers gaily dancing say stay a little while
Throwing gifts of perfume brings a tender smile

Jesus with your hand in mine I will tread the glade
At last I understand why the world was made
Messages from roses, all creatures great and small
To help me when I stumble, to hold me when I fall

Vie En Rose

INFORMATION

We hope you have enjoyed reading this book - and that you will continue to enjoy it in the coming years.

If you like reading and writing poetry drop us a line, or give us a call, and we'll send you a free information pack.

Write to :-

Triumph House Information
Remus House
Coltsfoot Drive
Woodston
Peterborough
PE2 9JX
(01733) 898102